LIGHT
and shade

Lighting up your life –
25 easy transformations

LIGHT
and shade

Lighting up your life –
25 easy transformations

STEWART AND SALLY WALTON

PHOTOGRAPHY BY GRAHAM RAE
STYLING BY CATHERINE TULLY

LORENZ BOOKS
NEW YORK • LONDON • SYDNEY • BATH

This edition published in 1996 by Lorenz Books
an imprint of Anness Publishing Limited
Administrative Office: 27 West 20th Street
New York, NY 10011

Lorenz books are available for bulk purchase for sales promotion and for premium use. For
details write or call the manager of special sales, Lorenz Books, 27 West 20th Street,
New York, 10011; (212) 807-6739

Produced by Anness Publishing Limited
1 Boundary Row
London SE1 8HP

ISBN 1 85967 128 4

Publisher: Joanna Lorenz
Senior Editor: Clare Nicholson
Photographer: Graham Rae
Stylist: Catherine Tully
Designer: Caroline Reeves

Printed in Singapore by
Star Standard Industries Pte Ltd

CONTENTS

INTRODUCTION

There are so many creative ways to use light decoratively at home. All you need is the igniting spark of inspiration to get you going. A good starting point is to take a look at the lights that are already in your home. Some of the quick projects shown in this book could be just what is needed to give them an injection of style. A glazed ceramic lamp base could be given a rough stone texture or wrapped in coils of rope, and a varnished wooden candlestick light might look better in faded country antique colors, or more sophisticated if gilded.

Shades can be glamorized with glass bead fringing or given an ethnic look with stamped, earthy-colored patterns. Striped shades are always effective, and different colors can be used to create different moods. Patterns can be cut out of paper shades to allow shafts of light to escape, and tin shades can be drilled or pierced for a similar effect.

Wall lights that offend can be replaced with small spotlights which can then be creatively shaded with unusual objects such as baskets, fans, colanders or perhaps a custom-made sculpture of wire mesh, patchworked with different textures. Each idea that appeals to you among the following projects will spark off another one of your own.

If you are starting afresh in a new home or redecorating from scratch, consider the positioning of your existing light fixtures right from the start. Lighting should never be an afterthought. It is one of the home decorator's most dynamic tools, so use it creatively and enjoy the illuminating experience.

QUICK DECORATIVE EFFECTS

Above: This lamp shade has been decorated using a high-density foam rubber stamp, inked in two colors with a paint roller.

A plain lamp shade is like a blank canvas just waiting for the artist's creative touch. The best type for decorating is a simple shape made of plain smooth fabric or thick paper. If you are experimenting, it is best to use the least expensive type because you will feel less restricted knowing that failure won't cost a fortune. A fabulous result can always be repeated on a better quality shade.

Stencils, stamps or freehand brushstrokes can be used to paint colorful motifs and patterns. The simplest are often the most effective, and it is worth trying a light behind the shade to see how the pattern will show up at night. Try a pattern of dots, zigzags and stripes in earthy colors on a cream background to give an African look, or use black silhouettes on a terracotta-colored shade for a classical Greek effect. Sky-blue stripes on a white shade look really fresh and burnt-orange patterns on a yellow shade seem like instant sunshine. Before you embark on the whole shade, first paint a small area to check the effect on the fabric or paper.

Cut out pattern shapes from the shade with a sharp scalpel. The stars on page 30, for example, look spectacular with the light shining through. As an alternative to cutting a star shape out of the lamp shade, cut out only the outer part of the shape. Lift the points to allow just a flash of light to shine through. A hole punch can be adjusted to make different-sized holes as decoration along the top and bottom edges of a shade in combination with a larger cut design around the middle section. Try a simple punched border laced with raffia, ribbon or string in a contrasting color.

Photocopy a black-and-white image, then make copies to cut out for a decoupaged shade. Use wallpaper paste to stick the photocopied cutouts in place on a paper shade, then apply clear varnish to give a smooth finish and prevent any curling at the edges. Another good alternative is to use your lamp shade as an unusual photograph album. Stick old photographs all around the outside of a pale-colored shade in a patchwork design. They will fade with age, creating a nostalgic feel.

Above: To achieve this gold-leaf effect, paint a small area of the shade with slightly diluted white glue. Lay a sheet of leaf on top and rub with a stencil brush. Brush off any excess. Repeat the process until the shade is covered.

Above: Pins, needles, scalpels and small sharp-pointed scissors can be used to cut intricate patterns out of paper lamp shades. On this shade, the pineapple has been used since it is a symbol of hospitality and was a great favorite with folk artists.

Above: Shells have been pinpricked into this lamp shade from the inside to give a raised effect.

INSTANT ENHANCEMENTS

Above: These plastic beads and jewels have transformed this plain shade into a fun, brightly-colored lamp that would be ideal for a child's bedroom.

Lamp shades seem to cry out for enhancements and armed with a glue gun and a plain shade, you can really go to town. Almost anything can be stuck onto the surface or dangled from the edge. The range of trimmings on the market today is very extensive, and you can buy fringes, beads and baubles to suit every style of shade and type of decor.

Large shades look particularly striking dressed up with upholstery fringing and matching tassels glued around the bottom edge. Many specialty shops and department stores sell beautiful ribbons in shot taffeta and silk that can be added as swags and bows. Milliner's velvet is another good alternative that can be finished off with fake flowers or fruit.

Smaller shades can be dressed up with finer decorations such as borders of beadwork or fine fringing. A border of bold buttons looks good in primary colors and wooden or leather buttons have a solid country feel.

Natural "found" materials like seashells, driftwood or sea glass from the beach make great edgings, too. A row of hanging mussel shells or small pine cones would make a very unusual fringe. With all of these ideas for decorating lamp shades, it will look very striking if you decorate the lamp base with ornaments to match. If the lamp base has a smooth varnished surface, rub it very lightly with sandpaper before gluing objects on.

You can alter the hard-edged shape of a shade by covering it with another material, such as colored net (tulle) or draped cheesecloth, both of which allow plenty of light through. It is best to use lightweight fabrics for this reason, otherwise the effect will be lost when the bulb is lit. Even a string bag can be pulled over a shade to create an interesting texture. Just trim it to the edges and use the glue gun to secure it.

There are so many different ways to dress up lamp shades that the only problem is knowing when to stop! If you are not careful, you will find yourself trying to improve every lamp shade in sight.

Above: Here a small lamp shade has been swathed in muslin, which allows plenty of light through. An even simpler option is to drape a beautiful scarf over a lamp shade. However, be careful not to let the material get too close to the light bulb since this will become very hot.

Above: This plain shade was given a country feel by lacing ribbon around the edges. Small pieces of natural-colored ribbon were frayed then randomly cross stitched onto the shade.

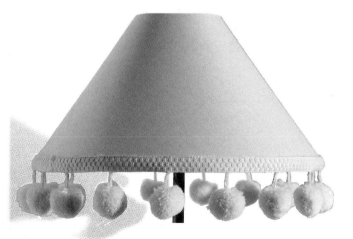

Left: This square lamp shade frame has been hung with double lengths of taffeta ribbon which have then been mitered where the ends meet and weighed down with gold beads.

Above: This cream lamp shade has been dressed up by gluing complementary colored braiding to the edge.

UNUSUAL EASY IDEAS

Sometimes it is good to take a fresh look at lighting and cast aside the obvious in favor of the unusual. A good starting point is to buy a small spotlight, either for wall mounting or a freestanding one for a table top. Then look around for a suitably inventive shade or cover for it: baskets, buckets, goldfish bowls, boxes, flowerpots, fabric, paper or folded cardboard can all be turned into unusual table lights. For walls, the principle is the same. Experiment with fans, draped fabrics, suspended paper, photographs, metal grids, parasols or lace panels; if you can hang it up and shine a light from behind it, then give it a try.

Be daring but always consider safety first and foremost, making sure any shading device stays clear of the light bulb at all times. Choose a low watt bulb for this sort of lighting – 40-watt bulbs generate a low heat, making them ideal for wall lights.

Above: Strings of Christmas lights are powered through transformers which reduce the bulb heat to a minimum, allowing them to be left on over a long period of time. A bundle of these lights arranged in a goldfish bowl lined with crumpled paper make a great table lamp. Try twisting them up poles or around picture frames for a touch of fun in a contemporary room setting.

Left: Disguise a utilitarian wall spotlight with this unusual paper shade. Oriental import shops sell these delicate paper cuts in all sorts of patterns ranging from birds and flowers to children playing games. The paper cuts are sold protected by thin paper folders which are linked together to make a large sheet which can then be paper clipped in front of a wall light.

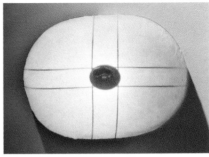

Above: Chicken wire, sieves, colanders and domed fly screens (shown here) all make good lamp shades and can be lined with tissue paper for a soft glowing effect.

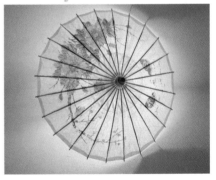

Above: Two fans attached to a wall with spotlights behind them create a very dramatic effect.

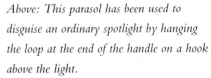

Above: This parasol has been used to disguise an ordinary spotlight by hanging the loop at the end of the handle on a hook above the light.

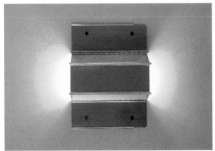

Left: The small aluminum screens sold by sporting goods stores to shield small stoves make stylish wall lights.

DECORATIVE EFFECTS ON BASES

Above: Bands of bright color have been used to emphasize the turned shape of this lamp base and the red shade complements the bright colors.

Treat your tired old lamp base to a makeover with a paint effect or some applied decoration, or customize a plain new base to give it an exclusive designer look.

A varnished wooden lamp base can be stripped down to bare wood, then painted with a bright base coat and a softer top coat. Rub back the paint with wire wool to reveal flashes of color and natural wood underneath. Or, you could use bands of flat bright color to emphasize the turned shape. Try out a paint effect such as tortoiseshell, crackle glaze or stenciling, then finish it off with a shade which complements the different-colored base.

Gilding used to be a special skill, but hobby kits can now be used to provide the ultimate illusion of turning wood into gold. Flashes of gold can be applied by rubber stamping gold size onto a surface and pressing gold leaf onto it. When the excess is brushed off, you will be left with a golden pattern. Other metal finishes to try are verdigris, a blue-green powdery effect, and rust, which can be simulated by adding sand and white glue to two shades of orangy-brown paint.

A glue gun is the essential tool for adding surface decoration to bases because of the instant bond achieved since the hot glue cools on contact. This frees you to work on vertical surfaces without having to wait for glue to set. Lamp bases can be completely covered with rope or string, or they can be partially decorated with beads, fringing or twisted braids.

Decoupage can be used too, and it doesn't have to be a traditional floral style. Any printed image can be cut out, stuck down on the base and varnished. Look out for old engraved illustrations of household wares or raid your childhood stamp collection and cover a base with stamp patchwork.

Above: A smooth-glazed pottery lamp base can be given the texture of rough stone by covering it with a mixture of white glue, sand and latex paint.

Above: Gilding has been used to transform this ordinary lamp base into one that will look very impressive in any setting.

Above: Mirrored mosaic is the perfect accompaniment for any kind of lighting. The mirror pieces have been stuck on with tile adhesive and the gaps in between have been painted with gold paint.

CANDLELIGHT

Candles provide a sense of occasion, perhaps because in recent years they were used only for birthday cakes, Christmas trees and dinner parties. Now they are used often, but they retain their special atmospheric quality. Candlelight moves, flickers and glows, concentrating its brilliance around the flame and leaving all but its immediate surroundings bathed in shadow. There are many different types of candle holder for sale, ranging from the simplest utilitarian candlestick to wonderfully decorative hanging chandeliers that hold enough candles to light up a banquet hall.

Wall sconces have the advantage of not needing to be positioned where electric wiring is fitted and a simple masonry nail is enough to hold them securely. They prevent a room from shrinking in the candlelight by reflecting images; indeed when candles were the only available light source, sconces used to have inlaid polished tin, glass or mirror reflectors.

Look out for old wooden branched center lights since these can be adapted to hold candles. Remove the electrical wiring and use the cups of the light fittings as candle holders. Paint the frame and decorate it with ribbons and dangling decorations. Candle lamps with shades have a formality that suits elegant living or dining rooms. If you are installing a hanging chandelier, make sure that the ceiling beam can stand the weight, since they are heavy.

Above: Star-shaped lanterns are ideal for drafty hallways.

Right: Plain and punched tin lanterns and hurricane lamps can be hung from brackets, shelves or ceiling hooks, and there are many different types to choose from. Look out for African or Indian imports for an exotic touch.

Above: One of the most restful pleasures in life is bathing by candlelight. The warm glowing flames create a sensuous, relaxing atmosphere which helps stresses and strains float away.

Above right: This inexpensive metal chandelier made in Sweden brings a real sense of style to the corner of a living room. Moroccan tin lanterns confirm that folk-art treasures can be found all around the globe.

Above: Candle holders are sometimes incorporated in the design of other practical items. This fruit basket with three integral candle holders is ideal for a country kitchen.

STAINED-GLASS BULB

Light bulbs can be painted in jewel colors to look like little illuminated stained-glass balls. Ordinary light bulbs can be used, but the one shown here is a large 60-watt decorative globe bulb. Painted bulbs deserve to be shown off, so hang them low over a table with a shallow shade that will not distract attention from the pretty patterns cast by the colored shapes. Special glass paints are available from art-and-craft shops, and a little paint will go a long way.

YOU WILL NEED

- ◆ light bulb
- ◆ waterproof marker pen
- ◆ 3 pieces of cardboard
- ◆ scalpel and cutting mat
- ◆ strip of corrugated cardboard
- ◆ sticky tape
- ◆ glass paints: pink, green, yellow, blue and black
- ◆ paintbrushes

1 Draw a circle on each piece of cardboard, one the size of the widest part of the bulb, one the size of the center of the star design and the third in between the two. Cut out the circles. Slip each piece of cardboard in turn over the bulb and draw a guideline on the glass where each sits. Carefully draw the guidelines for the rest of the design.

2 Roll up the corrugated cardboard strip to make a base for supporting the bulb. Secure the roll with sticky tape.

3 Begin painting the top of the bulb. Start with the central dot and radiating arms of the star. Support your painting hand with your free hand to steady it.

4 Working carefully, fill in all the different parts of the design, applying more than one coat where necessary to build up the color. Allow the paint to dry. Then paint a thick black line around each color section to give a stained-glass effect.

A SHADE ORIENTAL

The global supermarket is now well and truly a part of our lives, and strings of brightly colored fabric birds from the orient have become as familiar to us as imports from closer to home. The lamp shade made here is a combination of Chinese bamboo weaving and Indian textile work put together in a way that is reminiscent of an Australian bush hat! The lamp shade looks best when hung low over a kitchen table or anywhere that needs light combined with vibrant color.

YOU WILL NEED

- string of Indian hanging textile birds
- scissors
- needle
- embroidery thread
- assorted beads
- bamboo lamp shade
- scrap-paper measuring strip

1 Cut the retaining bead off the string of hanging birds, and remove the cord to separate the birds and beads.

2 Thread the needle with about 12in of embroidery thread and tie a bead at the end of the thread. Push the needle up through the existing hole in one of the birds, and then thread on three more beads.

3 Attach the bird to the shade, allowing it to hang down three finger widths from the rim. Divide the rim into ten equal sections, and attach a bird at each division.

4 Attach an inner row of birds one-third of the way up the shade. Position them so that they hang between the birds on the outer row and at a slightly higher level. Use a paper measuring strip to calculate the thread lengths required.

STRETCH-CLOTH SHADE

Stretch cloth is a knitted fabric which, although originally designed for wrapping meat, is generally used for cleaning. It can, however, be put to more interesting use. Here, it has been used to cover an ordinary lamp shade frame by opening out the tube and pulling it down over the frame. A second layer of fabric covers the first and is attached so that the edges roll over. Then a third layer is pulled over this.

YOU WILL NEED

- lamp shade frame
- tape measure
- scissors
- 1½yd sheer, stretch cloth
- straight pins
- needle
- thread, to match the cloth
- embroidery needle
- yellow embroidery thread

1 Cut a length of cloth three times the height of the frame. Pull the cloth down over the frame, so that you have just enough to roll under the bottom. Cut the rest off.

2 Divide the remaining cloth in two. Then pull a second length of cloth down over the frame. Catch the middle of each side along the top and bottom of the frame, and pin. The unpinned edges will roll up. Sew the first layer and the pinned section of the second layer to the frame.

3 Pull the third length of cloth down over the frame, and pin all around the top and bottom edges. Stitch to secure.

4 Cross stitch around the top and bottom of the cloth shade with a length of yellow embroidery thread to add a subtle finishing touch to the shade.

GILDED-PAPER PATCHWORK

Give two plain lamp shades a glittering new look by covering them in paper patchwork in two different styles. Although the arrangement and techniques for each shade differ slightly, they have enough in common to be used as a stunning pair. The paper can be any type that is not too thick: newsprint, tissue paper, brown wrapping paper, photocopied typescript, sheet music or fine woven papers. Make a feature of ragged edges, and avoid a regular, neat finish. The very special linking finishing touch is added with flashes of brilliant gold. The leaf used here is called Dutch metal. It is applied in the same way as gold leaf but at a fraction of the cost. If you have never done any gilding before, these shades are a good starting point since a perfect, even finish is not required.

YOU WILL NEED

CUT-PAPER PATCHWORK

- ◆ selection of interesting paper materials: corrugated cardboard, colored scrim ribbon, brown wrapping paper, handmade papers, paper mesh
- ◆ scissors
- ◆ plain cream fabric or paper lamp shade
- ◆ premixed wallpaper paste or white glue
- ◆ household paintbrushes for applying glue, an artist's paintbrush and a firm-bristled brush
- ◆ gold size
- ◆ Dutch metal leaf
- ◆ soft cloth

TORN-PAPER PATCHWORK

- ◆ selection of interesting paper materials: photocopied typescript, paper mesh, brown wrapping paper, handmade fiber paper, handmade paper, tracing paper
- ◆ shellac
- ◆ household paintbrushes for applying stainers and glue, and an artist's paintbrush
- ◆ denatured alcohol
- ◆ water-based stain: a natural wood shade
- ◆ plain cream paper lamp shade
- ◆ premixed wallpaper paste or white glue
- ◆ gold size
- ◆ Dutch metal leaf
- ◆ soft cloth

Cut-paper patchwork

1 Cut out "squares" from the different materials. Make them roughly equally sized, but trim them at an angle on both sides to taper slightly to fit the shade's conical shape.

2 Try out various combinations of texture and color until you are happy with the arrangement. Apply a coat of wallpaper paste or white glue to the backs of the shapes, and stick them in place on the shade. Butt them against each other to form a solid patchwork.

3 Paint "stitches" of gold size to link the squares together. Think of bold patchwork stitching, and make the lines vertical on the top and bottom of the squares and horizontal on the sides.

4 Cut the Dutch metal leaf into strips, with the backing sheet still in place. Gently press the leaf onto the tacky gold-size stitches.

5 Use a firm-bristled brush to clean away all the excess leaf, leaving just the stitches. Burnish with a soft cloth.

Torn-paper patchwork

1 Tear the different papers into similarly sized shapes, leaving the edges ragged and uneven.

2 Tint one-third of the shapes with shellac. It is fast-drying and will make the papers stiffer and also slightly transparent. The brush will need cleaning with denatured alcohol.

3 Tint another third of the paper shapes using water-based stain and allow them to dry. ⟶

4 Arrange the shapes on the shade, overlapping them in places and making a feature of the ragged edges. Practice with different arrangements until you are happy with the result.

5 Apply wallpaper paste or white glue to the backs of the shapes, and stick them onto the shade, using the stained shapes first. Space them wide apart to begin with and build up gradually.

6 Fill in gaps with the untinted papers.

7 Paint a ½in border line around the top and bottom of the shade with gold size.

8 Cut the sheets of Dutch metal leaf into strips, with the backing sheet still in place.

9 Press the strips against the tacky gold size along both edges. Overlap them when you need to. The leaf will only stick to the sized sections.

10 Rub off any excess leaf, and burnish with a soft cloth.

Opposite: The wonderful shine produced by Dutch metal leaf just can't be equaled by gold paints, creams or powders.

S K E W B A L D - P A T T E R N E D   S H A D E

A skewbald pattern is perhaps the boldest of animal-skin prints and always makes a strong style statement. It is adaptable enough to be used in a contemporary, minimalist room, a child's bedroom, a study, or to go back to its roots in a Tex-Mex ranch style.

Brown wrapping paper makes good stencils; the shapes need to be irregular to imitate the unique character of a skewbald pattern.

YOU WILL NEED
- ◆ felt-tipped pen
- ◆ brown wrapping paper
- ◆ scalpel
- ◆ cutting mat
- ◆ spray adhesive
- ◆ plain fabric lamp shade
- ◆ brown acrylic paint
- ◆ paintbrush
- ◆ glue gun with all-purpose glue sticks
- ◆ brown fringing

1 Draw irregular cloudlike shapes on brown wrapping paper. You need several small ones and a bigger one. Keep the shapes curved. Use a scalpel to cut out the stencils.

2 Spray the backs of the stencils very lightly with adhesive and arrange them on the shade. Position the large shape to overlap the rim.

3 Stencil the brown shapes onto the shade, working inward from the edges and making sure the paint gets into the weave of the fabric.

4 Stencil the larger shape right up against any edging strip or over the rim of the shade. The pattern will appear more natural if you do it this way. Use the glue gun to stick the fringing around the bottom rim.

STARRY NIGHT

Capture a small piece of the midnight sky by making this cutout lamp shade. Choose the deepest of blue shades, since the effect will be best if the light is completely blocked except by the star-shaped holes. The stars should be ¹/₂–³/₄in wide; any smaller or larger and the effect will be lost. Use a very sharp scalpel to cut the points of the stars, and always cut from the top of a point toward the middle. The lamp shade looks spectacular at night, but you can get a similar effect by day if you add a decoration of raised metal stars. Available from accessory stores, these have spikes at the back that are pressed through the shade and folded flat on the inside.

YOU WILL NEED

- ◆ white paper
- ◆ pencil
- ◆ scissors
- ◆ spray adhesive
- ◆ navy-blue paper lamp shade
- ◆ cutting mat
- ◆ scalpel
- ◆ metal star studs
- ◆ high-density foam rubber

2 Rest the shade on the cutting mat, and cut out the stars using a scalpel. Working from the right side of the shade, cut through any threads that remain and gently push the stars inward to remove them.

1 Using the template on page 93, draw 50 stars on white paper. Cut the paper into small squares with one star in the center of each. Lightly spray the backs of the squares with adhesive, and stick them inside the shade. Arrange them randomly rather than spacing them symmetrically.

3 Make sure that the spikes on the backs of the metal stars are straight, otherwise they will not penetrate the shade. Hold a piece of dense foam rubber inside the shade to give you something to push against. Then press the stars through and fold the spikes over at the back.

INCA BIRD PRINT

Make an impression on a tall conical lamp shade by stamping it all over with a strong printed pattern. The shade used here is made of thin, mottled cardboard that resembles vellum and which casts a warm glow when the lamp is lit. The stamp is based on an Inca bird design that is bold enough for a beginner to cut and is even enhanced by a slightly rough cutting style.

YOU WILL NEED

- ◆ white paper
- ◆ spray adhesive
- ◆ high-density foam rubber
- ◆ scalpel
- ◆ white glue
- ◆ flat plate
- ◆ premixed wallpaper paste
- ◆ golden brown and darker brown premixed watercolor paint in dropper bottle
- ◆ small paint roller
- ◆ conical paper lamp shade

1 Photocopy the motif from page 92. Spray the back of the copy lightly with adhesive and stick it onto the foam rubber. Cut around the shape with the scalpel and scoop away the background so that the motif stands alone.

2 Put about a teaspoon of white glue onto the plate. Add a similar amount of wallpaper paste and a few drops of golden-brown paint, and mix well. Run the paint roller through the mixture to coat it evenly and use it to coat the stamp.

3 Print the motif on the shade by pressing the stamp onto the surface and then removing it directly. The wallpaper paste makes the paint gelatinous, leaving an interesting texture when you lift the stamp.

4 Add a few drops of the darker paint to the mixture and stamp more motifs on the shade.

TRIO OF PAINTED SHADES

Nothing could be quicker, easier or cheaper than painting squiggles, spots or flecks of color on a few plain lamp shades to add a touch of individuality to any room.

The three shades shown here have each been made using a different decorative technique. All are fun to do, and only the black-and-white stripes require a steady hand. Use plain fabric shades and experiment with color, using it to reinforce an existing decorating theme or to add a spark of brilliance to a monotonous color scheme.

YOU WILL NEED
BLOTTING-PAPER EFFECT
- plain fabric lamp shade
- paintbrushes
- bright-blue premixed watercolor paint
- dropper bottle

PAINTED-LINE EFFECT
- cardboard
- cutting mat
- plain fabric lamp shade
- scalpel
- metal ruler
- black acrylic paint
- paintbrushes: large square-tipped and small

FLECKED EFFECT
- plain fabric lamp shade
- cardboard
- pencil
- scalpel
- cutting mat
- toothbrush
- water-based acrylic, poster, watercolor or gouache paints: yellow ocher, brick-red and cream
- paintbrush

Blotting-paper effect

1 Dampen the whole outer surface of the fabric lamp shade with water, using a large paintbrush.

2 Fill the dropper bottle with blue paint, and squeeze it gently to deposit one small drop onto the shade. Watch the effect as the blot spreads so that you can judge where to position the next drop.

3 Turn the lamp shade with your free hand and, as you do so, drop equal amounts of paint, spaced fairly evenly all around the shade.

4 Fill the spaces between the blots with a more random pattern of differently sized dots, but be careful not to cover all the original lamp shade color completely.

5 Holding the lamp shade from the inside with your free hand and resting your painting hand on the work surface, paint the top and bottom rims solid blue.

Painted-line effect

1 Cut a right-angled piece of cardboard with one edge the same length as the height of the shade. Angle the other side to make it easy to hold.

2 Hold the square-edged cardboard up against the shade and paint a wide squiggle to the right of it, using the large brush. After each squiggle, move the cardboard along; this will ensure that you paint vertically and don't slide off in one direction, which is easily done when painting a shape like this.

3 Paint fine squiggly lines between the fatter ones, using the small paintbrush. Support the wrist of your painting hand with your free hand to keep it steady.

4 Finish off the lamp shade by painting the top and bottom rims with a solid black line.

Flecked effect

1 Place the shade upside down on the piece of cardboard, and draw around the inside of the top rim. Cut this circle out, just slightly larger than the drawn pencil line, and place it on top of the shade to prevent any paint from dripping on to the inside.

2 Place the shade on a protected work surface. Fill the toothbrush with the yellow ocher paint. Then draw your thumb backward over the bristles to fleck the lamp shade with color. Try to get a fine, even covering, but allow the background to show through.

3 Clean the toothbrush, then dip it into the brick-red paint. Use the brush at an angle to make randomly placed wedge-shaped marks at different angles over the flecked pattern. Don't try for a regular pattern: look at the example to judge the effect you are after.

4 To finish the decoration, clean the toothbrush, then apply the cream paint in the same way. It may not show up much but when the lamp is lit at night, all will be revealed.

Opposite: These three lamp shades have been decorated to suit a modern interior. Vary the colors and use more muted tones for a country look.

LIZARD-SKIN CONE

There are some fabulous textured papers around that are just perfect for making lamp shades. Lizard-skin-effect paper is a good example. It looks great by day and even better when lit. Here, the fabric from an old lamp shade was carefully removed and used as a pattern for the lizard skin.

YOU WILL NEED

♦ old lamp shade, 7¼in diameter
♦ sheet of lizard-skin paper
♦ pen
♦ ruler
♦ scissors
♦ hole punch
♦ small piece of cardboard
♦ double-sided tape
♦ night-light holder
♦ needle
♦ thick black thread
♦ white glue

1 Dismantle the old shade, and lay the fabric on the reverse of the lizard-skin paper. Draw around the shape, extending the narrowing lines to make a long, narrow cone. The height of this one is 11in, the narrow end curve is 6½in and the wide base curve is 24in. Carefully cut out the shape with a pair of scissors.

2 Using a hole punch, make a row of equally spaced holes along the bottom edge. Place a piece of cardboard behind the paper to prevent creasing.

3 Join the sides of the shade with double-sided tape, overlapping them by ½in and making sure the night-light holder will fit inside the narrow end of the shade.

4 Place the old frame in position, and stitch the bottom edge of the shade to the frame. For decorative effect, make the stitches at a 45-degree angle. Trim the narrow end of the shade to fit snugly inside the night-light holder. Paint inside the holder with white glue, and fit it over the end of the shade.

TRIMMED SHADES

Turn a plain-colored lamp shade into a completely wacky extrovert by adding a dangling fringe of trimmings. Almost anything nonperishable that will thread can be used – the choice is yours. Check out the toy store, especially the impulse selection, where bright beads, miniature dolls and fluorescent-plastic balls are all waiting to be snapped up.

YOU WILL NEED

♦ plain conical lamp shade
♦ square of paper or cardboard
♦ pencil
♦ T-square
♦ hole punch
♦ strong thread
♦ needle
♦ selection of beads, toys, baubles, etc.
♦ glue (optional)

1 Place the lamp shade on a square of paper or cardboard, and draw around the bottom edge in pencil.

2 Use a T-square to divide the circle into eight equal segments.

3 Replace the shade on the paper or cardboard, and mark the divisions around the edge in pencil.

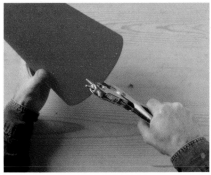

4 Use the hole punch to make eight small holes about $1/2$in up from the edge of the shade, in line with the pencil marks.

5 Tie a bead at the end of the thread. Then thread on a selection of your chosen baubles and beads.

6 Attach to the shade by sewing the thread through one of the punched holes several times, finishing with a secure knot. An extra bead can be glued to the edge of the shade to cover the thread. Decorate the rest of the shade in the same way.

Above and right: This painted green lamp shade has been decorated with paper ties making it ideal for an office light. To make the shade, punch a ring of holes around the top and bottom with a hole punch. Then thread the paper ties onto the shade.

PRIMARY PLASTIC

Thin sheets of opaque, colored plastic, which are available from art supply shops, make excellent lamp shade materials. The edges can be cut decoratively with no need for seaming and the plastic does not require a supporting frame.

YOU WILL NEED
- ◆ brown wrapping paper
- ◆ spray adhesive
- ◆ sheet of red or yellow plastic
- ◆ craft knife
- ◆ cutting mat
- ◆ pen
- ◆ ruler
- ◆ broad cloth tape
- ◆ masking tape
- ◆ scrap of wood
- ◆ drill with twist bit
- ◆ nuts and bolts
- ◆ shade carrier

Red shade

1 Enlarge the template on page 92 on a photocopier, and transfer the shape onto the brown paper. Spray the back with adhesive, and stick it onto the red sheet of plastic. Cut out the shade using a sharp craft knife.

2 Make a cardboard template for the sawtooth pattern. Place it on the edge of the brown-paper pattern, still attached to the plastic sheet, and draw around it to form a continuous zigzag line.

3 Cut out the sawtooth border, using the craft knife. Cut toward the outside edge each time.

4 Remove the paper. Then overlap the two long edges of the shade and secure with cloth tape. Place a strip of masking tape along this seam. Place the wood block behind the seam. Then drill three holes through the plastic only. Peel off the tape and screw in the nuts and bolts. ➤

Yellow shade

1 Enlarge the template on page 93 on a photocopier and transfer the shape onto the brown paper. Spray the back with adhesive, and stick it onto the yellow sheet of plastic. Place on the cutting mat, and cut out the shade using a sharp craft knife.

3 Using a ruler, mark five equal divisions along the seam. Place a wooden block behind the seam, and carefully drill a hole through the plastic at each mark.

2 Overlap the two long edges of the shade, and secure with a strip of cloth tape. Then place a strip of masking tape along this seam.

4 Start peeling off the tape at the top of the shade, and screw in a nut and bolt each time a drilled hole is exposed.

Right: To attach the shades to a lamp base, you will need to screw a shade carrier onto the lamp fixture. Shade carriers come in a range of heights from 4–12in.

RAFFIA STANDARD LAMP

Standard lamps provide the perfect overhead light to read by, without diminishing the atmosphere of a room the way bright central ceiling lights can. Placing one in the corner will mean that someone can use it to see what they are doing while the rest of the room can be dimmed for watching television or general relaxation. Here, a turned-wood standard lamp has been enclosed in a sheath of raffia that is finished off by a "thatched" base that resembles a very clean chimney sweep's brush.

YOU WILL NEED
- ◆ turned-wood standard lamp
- ◆ rubber bands
- ◆ several bunches of natural-colored raffia
- ◆ scissors
- ◆ colored raffia

1 Place a rubber band at the bottom of the pole. Unravel the raffia, and cut a handful of 15in lengths. Fold the lengths in half and tuck them under the band, so that the band holds them in place just below the fold. Continue inserting folded lengths until the base is completely covered.

2 Wind a strand of raffia around the rubber band several times, and tie it tightly to hold the raffia base in place.

3 Place a rubber band around the top of the lamp. Unravel the raffia, and tuck bunches under the band until the pole is covered. About 10in down from the band, wind a strand of raffia around the pole. Repeat at intervals down the pole.

4 At the base, tuck the raffia into the top of the base raffia, then bind to cover the join. Trim any loose ends. For contrast, cover the plain raffia bindings with colored raffia.

CORRUGATED LAMP BASE

Corrugated cardboard has sculptural qualities that elevate it from a mere packaging material. Its construction, with one smooth and one ridged side, means that it can be rolled into even, tubular shapes to make lamp bases. Corrugated cardboard is very lightweight so site the lamp where it is unlikely to be knocked over.

YOU WILL NEED

♦ roll of corrugated cardboard
♦ ruler
♦ scalpel
♦ cutting mat
♦ glue gun with all-purpose glue sticks
♦ pencil
♦ bottle-adaptor lamp fixture

1 Cut a $20^{1}/_{2}$ x $13^{3}/_{4}$in rectangle of cardboard and roll it lengthwise, leaving the center hollow for the lamp fixture. Glue the loose edge.

2 Cut a 53 x $1^{1}/_{2}$in rectangle from the cardboard. Measure in $7^{1}/_{4}$in from the top left corner, draw a line between this point and the bottom right corner and cut along this line. Apply glue to the square end and line it up with the column base. Wrap it around, gluing to hold the layers together. Keep the base flat.

3 Cut a $20^{1}/_{2}$ x $1^{1}/_{2}$in rectangle. Then glue and wrap it around the base to add extra stability.

4 Cut another 53 x $1^{1}/_{2}$in rectangle. Then glue and wrap this around the top of the column. Keep the top flat. Ask an electrician to install the bottle-adaptor lamp fixture and to wire it to a flex.

PICKLED LAMP BASE

One of the most effective ways of updating a dull lamp is to give the base a fashionable paint finish and add a fresh new shade. Look out for secondhand bargains in yard sales or thrift shops. Then give them new life with a special paint treatment. This turned-wood lamp base has been given a pickled look by applying and rubbing back two colors. The first, blue-gray coat of paint is rubbed off but remains in the grain and the grooves. The second coat of white paint is also sanded down, leaving a transparent, pickled look.

YOU WILL NEED

♦ plain turned-wood lamp base

♦ latex paints: blue-gray and white

♦ paintbrushes

♦ 2 cloths

♦ fine-grade sandpaper

1 Paint the bare wood with a coat of blue-gray paint.

3 Rub the raised parts of the lamp base with fine-grade sandpaper.

2 Before the paint has dried, rub it off with a cloth to leave some color in the grooves and grain. Allow to dry.

4 Paint the whole lamp base with white latex paint. Rub the paint off before it has dried, using another cloth, and allow to dry. Sand the raised parts to create the pickled look.

STRING-BOUND LAMP BASE

String-binding is a brilliant way to disguise a tired old lamp base or to dress up a cheap generic purchase. Look out for a lamp base with good proportions and a pleasing shape. You will have more fun if you choose a base that has an ugly pattern or a really unpleasant color, because you then have the satisfaction of seeing it disappear! There are many kinds of string to choose from, ranging from smooth, fine, waxy and white to fat, loose-weave brown twine, and all give different effects. You could even use colored nylon string.

YOU WILL NEED
- glue gun with all-purpose glue sticks
- china, glass or wooden lamp base
- ball of string
- scalpel or scissors

1 Heat the glue gun and apply a dot of hot glue below the flex on the bottom edge of the lamp base. Press the string in place. Apply a thin line of glue to the string and work it around the lamp base, keeping the string taut.

2 Wind the string up around the base, dotting it with glue in key positions to hold the rows tightly together. When you reach the flex, cut the string. Apply a dot of glue on the other side of the hole and start the winding again.

3 Continue winding and gluing, applying glue at intervals to hold the string in place. It is important to use enough glue when winding around concave shapes, as this is where sagging could occur.

4 At the top of the lamp base, apply an extra dot of glue and cut the string at an angle so that it lies flat.

ANGULAR WALL LIGHT

This wall light is a shade slotted over a standard mini-spotlight. The two halves of the shade are clamped together with two sprung paper clips on each side. Before fitting them together, cut a hole in the back piece to slot over the base of the spotlight. Make the hole the same size as the spotlight base so that it fits snugly and will not slip. Fit the back of the shade in position first, making sure that the bulb will be well clear of the plastic.

YOU WILL NEED

- brown wrapping paper
- pencil
- ruler and T-square
- scissors
- spray adhesive
- sheet of yellow plastic
- sheet of red plastic
- craft knife and cutting mat
- small spotlight fixture
- 4 small sprung paper clips

1 Enlarge the template on page 91 on a photocopier. Transfer the pattern twice onto brown wrapping paper. Cut out the two identical patterns, leaving a $3/4$in seam allowance all around the edges.

2 Spray the paper patterns with adhesive and stick one on each of the plastic sheets. Cut out the shapes and nick the ends of the fold lines, so that they will be obvious from both sides.

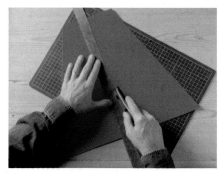

3 Remove the paper, then score the fold line, but do not cut more than the surface as you do it. Practice on the scraps first to get the pressure right.

4 Turn the sheets over and score the fold lines again, working between the nicks at each end. Fold up the shades. Cut a hole in the back shade to fit the spotlight base, place it over the spotlight, then attach the front piece with paper clips.

THE ROBERT CRAY BAND/STRONG PERSUADER   830

LEONARD COHEN   THE FUTURE

Ali Farka Toure with Ry Cooder   Talking Timbuktu

7321 1000 2   EDDI READER : MIRMAMA

bjork   debut   tplp 31 cd

The Complete Picture   the very best of deborah harry and blondie   CID 8013 09

BRUCE SPRINGSTEEN   BORN TO RUN

7599-26840-2   kd lang INGENUE   Sire Ye

THE VERY BEST OF WOODY GUTHRIE   M

MCD 10961   THE MAVERICKS · WHAT A CRYING SHAME

7243 8 39353 2 7   massive attack   protection

RED EYE RECORDS

Chrysalis   RUNRIG · SEARCHLIGHT ·

WOOD NIGHT SHADE

Wood veneer is a thin sheet shaved from a seasoned tree trunk and is sold by lumber merchants who supply furniture makers. Each sheet is unique, so choose the veneer with the best grain; it will look even better with light shining through it. The lamp shade shown here is made from flamed-ash veneer. The veneer hangs from a simple wooden frame but you could use a square picture frame (without the glass). Carefully remove one edge of the frame, thread on the curtain rings and glue the piece back. Suspend the veneer from the frame using clipped curtain rings. Hang the lamp shade on leather thongs or pieces of cord from a ceiling hook, with a pendant lamp fixture and bulb dangling inside it.

YOU WILL NEED

- ◆ 4 equal lengths of wooden dowel, mitered
- ◆ glue gun with all-purpose glue sticks
- ◆ curtain rings with clip attachments
- ◆ metal ruler
- ◆ scalpel
- ◆ sheet of wood veneer
- ◆ 4 equal lengths of cord or leather thongs

1 Join three pieces of dowel using the glue gun. Thread the rings onto the frame before gluing the last piece of dowel in place.

2 Measure the width of one side of the frame and, using the scalpel, cut four strips of veneer, one for each side. Make the length roughly twice the width. For a natural look, the pieces should not be precisely the same size.

3 Attach two clips to each sheet of veneer. Tie a cord or thong to each corner for hanging.

HANDMADE PAPER GLOBE

Covering an inflated balloon with papier mâché may not be the most original method, but the old ideas are often the best ones. You could use light tissue paper mixed with fibrous handmade paper scraps, layering dried flowers and leaves between them. Keep the same thickness across the top of the balloon, but allow it to taper off toward the tied end.

YOU WILL NEED
♦ balloon
♦ handmade paper scraps containing leaves and flower petals
♦ premixed wallpaper paste
♦ paintbrush
♦ cream or white tissue paper
♦ gauze or mesh
♦ pin
♦ scissors
♦ pendant lamp fixture
♦ cardboard ring
♦ all-purpose glue

1 Apply paste to small pieces of paper, and stick them onto the balloon in a random overlapping arrangement, beginning at the top.

2 Cover the top two-thirds of the balloon with three layers of paper, tissue paper and gauze or mesh. Leave until bone dry. This may take several days. Use a pin to pop the balloon and remove it from the shade.

3 Cut a small hole in the top of the shade. Use the light fixture as a guide.

4 Reinforce the hole by gluing a cardboard ring inside the shade. Screw the two halves of the pendant lamp fixture together, one on each side of the shade, and ask an electrician to wire the fixture to a flex.

CHICKEN-WIRE TORCH

This dramatic shade would look fabulous in an entrance hall, especially if teamed with an interesting paint finish. The basic shape is a cone, but the character relies on the layers of chicken wire interwoven with silver solder and copper wire. Spirals of wire, creating an unusual textural patchwork, hold the ragged torn paper in place.

The shade is hooked over a small wall spotlight via a slit cut into the wire mesh. The light picks up the colors of the silver solder and copper wire, adding a layer of brilliance on top of the grayish wire mesh, and shines through the different paper textures. The shade is very lightweight, but a coat of black latex paint applied to the base of the cone will add visual weight.

YOU WILL NEED

- ♦ 36 x 24in chicken wire
- ♦ needle-nose pliers
- ♦ hammer
- ♦ wire cutters
- ♦ small wall-light fixture
- ♦ silver solder
- ♦ copper wire
- ♦ 3 different, highly textured natural-weave papers
- ♦ black latex paint
- ♦ paintbrush
- ♦ screw and screwdriver

2 Roll the tube into a cone shape, so that the unattached end tapers down to a point. Pinch and twist the cut wire to hold the shape firm.

1 Roll the chicken wire into a tube with a 6$\frac{1}{2}$in diameter. Using the pliers, pinch and twist the cut edges to make a firm attachment at one end.

3 Compress the narrow end by hammering it on a hard surface. The wire mesh will scrunch up into a fairly solid mass.

4 Use the wire cutters to make a slit in the back of the cone, large enough to fit over the base of the wall-light fixture and lie flat against the wall.

6 Cut similar lengths of copper wire and weave them through the mesh. Here a zigzag pattern is used, but feel free to experiment.

8 Add a patchwork of chicken-wire pieces. The different depths of wire will be picked out and enhanced by the light when it is turned on.

5 Cut two 20in lengths of solder and weave them in and out of the mesh. Follow the shape of the cone, spiraling the wire upwards.

7 Wind copper wire around the outside of the cone, "sewing" it through the mesh in places.

9 Tear up the three sheets of paper. The edges should be rough and ragged. Tear some pieces into strips, and others into random shapes and rectangles.

10 Place the paper pieces randomly on the outside of the cone, and use spiraling strands of wire to bind them into place.

11 Use the needle-nose pliers to tweak and pinch the paper in places, so that it becomes a part of the structure instead of just sitting on the outside.

12 Carefully dry-brush black latex paint onto the narrow base of the torch, to give a matte-black charcoal finish.

13 Fit the torch over the wall-light fixture. Bend the mesh so that it fits snugly around the base and hammer a screw in the wall near the top of the torch to hold it in place.

Above: Chicken wire is cheap and surprisingly easy to work with. You can form the wire into elegant candle holders, candlesticks and shimmering bead domes.

Opposite: The torch shade can also be attached with the top angled slightly away from the wall. It must then be steadied by a wire attached to the screw fixture and the back of the torch.

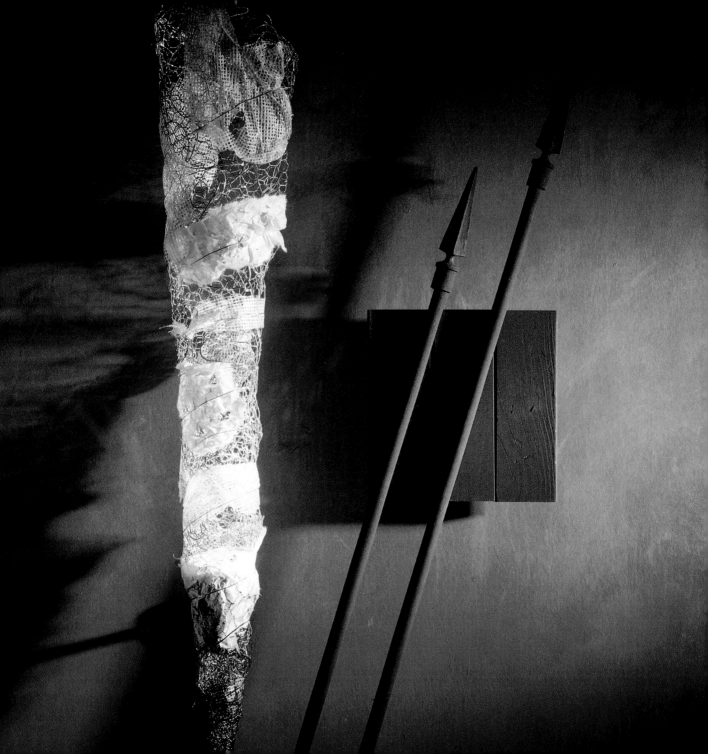

BIRD-CAGE LAMP SHADE

Designed to hang at eye level, bird cages

need very little adaptation to turn them

into unusual oriental-style shades.

This little wooden cage was made in the

Far East and, judging by the spacing of

the bars, cannot have been intended for a

real bird. Look out for wooden or bamboo

cages like this in gift shops, florist's or

import stores and, if necessary, adapt the

steps to suit the shape of the cage.

YOU WILL NEED

- ◆ small wooden or bamboo bird cage
- ◆ saw
- ◆ wire cutters
- ◆ tissue paper
- ◆ pencil and scissors
- ◆ premixed wallpaper paste
- ◆ paintbrush
- ◆ pendant lamp fixture

1 Using a saw and a strong pair of wire cutters, cut away the struts that make up the base of the cage.

2 Roll a sheet of tissue paper around the top section of the cage. Here it is conical. Mark the shape in pencil.

3 Cut out the shape. Apply wallpaper paste to the inside of the struts of the top section. Roll up the tissue paper. Then unfold it inside the cage, pressing it against the pasted struts to form a lining. Trim away any excess.

4 Cut out a rectangular tissue-paper shape to line the rest of the cage. Paste the inside of the struts. Then place the tissue paper inside the cage as a lining, as before. Allow to dry. Ask an electrician to attach the pendant lamp fixture and to wire it to a flex.

BENT-WIRE CHANDELIER

Magically crafted from a roll of wire, this delicate little chandelier was twisted and curled into shape with needle-nose pliers. Making it is so much fun that you will probably want to make a pair. Bonsai-training wire, sold in garden centers and by bonsai-tree specialists, was used here. Hang the chandelier from a chain and hook so that it can twist and turn in passing breezes.

YOU WILL NEED

- ◆ roll of silver bonsai-training wire
- ◆ wire cutters
- ◆ needle-nose pliers
- ◆ roll of gardening wire
- ◆ 4 self-tapping screws and screwdriver
- ◆ glue gun with all-purpose glue sticks
- ◆ 4 thumbtacks
- ◆ 4 night lights
- ◆ large sequins

1 Cut a 13³/₄in length of bonsai wire to make the first kidney-shaped curl. Hold the wire with your free hand and, gripping the end with the needle-nose pliers, shape it into a curl. Then, holding the first curl in your hand, curl the other end. Make a single curl from a smaller piece of wire.

2 Make two more single curls. Each branch is made of these four pieces.

3 Cut a 4³/₄in length of gardening wire and use it to bind the kidney-shaped curl and two of the single curls together at the point, as shown. Wind the wire around like a spring, to make a neat binding.

4 Screw a self-tapping screw into the center of the binding, leaving at least ¹/₂in protruding at the top.

5 Bind the third single curl to the back of the kidney shape, winding a length of gardening wire into a neat binding as before.

7 Cut a 20in length of bonsai wire for the central column. Twist one end into a decorative spiral and the other into a small hook for hanging.

9 Heat the glue gun, apply a dot of glue to one of the screwheads and immediately sit a thumbtack on it, pointing upward. Repeat with the three remaining screwheads.

6 Snip off the end of the gardening wire at an angle, close to the binding. Repeat the above steps to make the four branches.

8 Make two small, tight curls and bind them into the top end of the column, facing inward. Bind the four branches on to the central column, with the open side of the kidney-shaped curls facing upward.

10 Press a night light down on to each of the four points of the thumbtacks. Thread the large sequins on to the curls. Take care not to overdo this, as too many could detract from the elegance of the wire twists.

CHINESE LANTERN

This stick-and-cardboard lamp shade has a natural look by day, but lights up like a skyscraper at night. Sheets of corrugated cardboard can be bought in a range of colors from natural to fluorescent, and the wooden skewers can also be painted. You can use the lantern over any small table lamp or even a candle. If using a candle, place it in a secure holder.

YOU WILL NEED

♦ metal ruler, approximately 1¼in wide

♦ pen or pencil

♦ 13¾ x 10¼in sheet of corrugated cardboard

♦ cutting mat

♦ scalpel

♦ scrap paper

♦ gold spray paint

♦ package of wooden skewers

1 Using the width of the ruler as a spacer, draw vertical lines across the length of the cardboard.

2 Cut slits across the width of alternate columns, starting one in from the edge. Moving the ruler down a width at a time, continue cutting slits to the bottom of the cardboard.

3 Cut through the uncut rows in the same way, but starting with the ruler a half-drop down, so that the slits fall halfway between the first ones. Continue until the sheet is covered with a "brickwork" pattern of slits.

4 Protect your work surface with scrap paper, then spray the smooth side of the cardboard with gold paint.

5 Turn the cardboard over and weave the skewers in and out of the slits. Allow about 1in to protrude on one edge to give the shade legs to stand on.

7 Hold the two edges so that they overlap (with the smooth gold side inside), then weave the last skewer through the double thickness to join the lamp shade edges together.

6 Trim the last column to within ½in of the slits, so that the join will not be too bulky.

Right: Place the lantern over a table lamp or even a candle. With a candle, use a secure holder and place it at dead center to keep the flame away from the shade.

FLASHLIGHT LIGHT

A row of angled chrome spotlights adds the designer touch to any shelf display, but wiring and fixing them up can be an expensive undertaking. Here is a way to obtain an even better effect without spending a lot of money or even plugging anything into the electrical circuit! All you need is three cheap chrome flashlights, a length of towel rod with sockets, a few fixtures and an hour to spare.

YOU WILL NEED
- 3 small- or medium-sized chrome flashlights
- 3 small leather straps
- pencil
- hole punch
- 3 small jubilee clips
- chrome shower rod with 2 sockets
- screwdriver
- drill with masonry bit
- wall plugs and screws
- carpenter's level

1 Wrap a strap around a flashlight, and mark the point where the buckle spike should enter. This will assure you of a good tight fit. Mark the other straps in the same way.

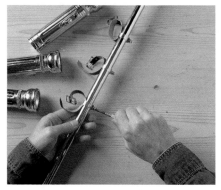

3 Slide the jubilee clips over the chrome rod, loop a strap through each one, then tighten the clips using a screwdriver, making sure that they are spaced at equal distances.

2 Punch a hole in each strap where you have marked it.

4 Fit the rod into the sockets and attach these to the wall. Use a carpenter's level to assure the rod is level before attaching. Buckle the flashlights to the rod.

STANDARD PAINT CANS

Necessity really is the mother of invention. This lamp was designed by a friend stuck in a remote village, who needed a good light to read by. The heavy lamp base is made from a large painted paint can filled with sand, while the shade is a smaller paint can drilled with a pattern of holes. The flex travels inside a curved copper plumbing pipe that is plunged into the sand.

The graceful bend of the copper piping can only be achieved using a special long spring used in the plumbing trade. You probably will need a plumber to bend the pipe for you. Ask an electrician to wire up the finished lamp for you.

YOU WILL NEED

- ♦ ½ gallon paint can
- ♦ paint stripper (optional)
- ♦ sandpaper
- ♦ cardboard
- ♦ scissors
- ♦ felt-tipped pen
- ♦ drill with size 6 twist metal bit
- ♦ hammer and nail (optional)
- ♦ metal file
- ♦ pendant lamp fixture
- ♦ matte-black latex paint
- ♦ paintbrush
- ♦ 1 gallon paint can
- ♦ string
- ♦ pipe bending spring
- ♦ 3yd copper pipe
- ♦ hacksaw
- ♦ rubber grommet
- ♦ silver sand to fill larger can

1 Strip off the paint or remove the label from the ½ gallon can, then rub down the surface with sandpaper. This will be the shade.

2 Cut a strip of cardboard the height of the can, then mark off three equal sections. Mark the other side in the same way but so that the marks fall halfway between the others. Use the strip to mark the drilling points around the can.

3 Drill holes through all the marked points. Drilling through metal is not difficult but, if the drill bit slips, dent each mark slightly with a hammer and nail before drilling.

5 Roughen up the outside of the can with the file, smoothing the drilled-hole edges and scratching a texture into the surface.

7 Drill a hole for the flex near the base of the can.

4 Find the center of the base of the can and drill four or five holes close together to make a larger hole. Use the end of a metal file to turn this into an even, circular hole that is the right size for the pendant lamp fixture.

6 Paint the outside of the 1 gallon paint can with the matte-black latex paint. Paint the lid separately.

8 The pipe bending spring will not be as long as the copper pipe so attach a piece of string to one end of the spring. Mark the string at intervals so that you will be able to tell how far down the copper pipe the spring is.

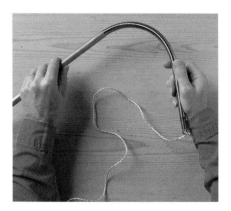

9 Insert the spring into the pipe and start to shape the top one third of the pipe into a semicircle. You will not be able to bend the pipe in one try so make small bends, bringing the spring back up the pipe as you work.

10 Saw off the straight section at the end, so that the curve will go into the can. Then attach the rubber grommet to the end of the copper pipe

11 At this stage, you need an electrician to thread the flex through the copper pipe and wire the fixture to it. The two halves of the fixture hold the shade between them. Drill a centrally positioned hole in the lid of the large can, to take the copper pipe. Fit the lid over the base of the pipe and feed the flex out through the hole drilled near the base.

Right: A simple way to make a dramatic light is to drill holes randomly around a paint can and then to light it with either a spotlight or a candle.

Opposite: The punched paint can will emit a wonderful dappled light.

12 Hold the lamp upright in the can and fill it with sand. Push the lid firmly on the can.

TRIPOD LIGHT

This contemporary-looking standard lamp appears quite delicate, but the tripod legs are very stable. The simplicity of the design makes it ideal for a Japanese-style room, particularly if a plain, natural fabric shade is fitted.

The lamp base is constructed from three pieces of wooden dowel that fit into angled holes drilled in a circle of wood. The shade is made by covering the frame with cheesecloth. The lamp is assembled by screwing a lamp fitting to the wooden disc, over a central hole through which the flex passes – ask an electrician to do this.

For a completely different effect, try painting the legs in various colors and using a vibrantly colored shade.

YOU WILL NEED

- ◆ soft cloth
- ◆ dark-oak wood stain
- ◆ 1yd lengths of wooden dowel
- ◆ pencil
- ◆ pair of compasses (optional)
- ◆ square piece of wood
- ◆ clamp
- ◆ 2 scraps of wood
- ◆ coping saw
- ◆ drill with twist bit
- ◆ scalpel
- ◆ wood glue
- ◆ tape measure
- ◆ large cylindrical shade frame
- ◆ dressmaker's scissors
- ◆ 3yd unbleached cheesecloth
- ◆ straight pins
- ◆ rust-colored 4-ply wool
- ◆ darning needle
- ◆ shade carrier

1 Using the cloth, rub the wood stain into the dowel.

2 Draw an 7¼in diameter circle on the square of wood, then clamp it ready for sawing, protecting it from the clamp with scraps of wood. Saw in from the edge at an angle and follow the curve with the blade. Move the wood round periodically, so that you always saw at a comfortable angle.

3 Using a drill bit that is marginally narrower than the dowel, drill three angled holes through the wood circle. If you hold the drill directly above the center, then tilt it slightly toward the edge, the angle will be correct. Drill a hole through the middle of the circle for the flex.

4 Shave the ends of the lengths of dowel slightly with a scalpel, apply wood glue and then push them into the drilled holes. Apply glue to the lengths of dowel where they intersect. Allow to dry.

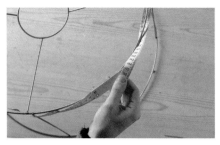

5 To cover the frame, measure around the circumference and height. Cut a double thickness of cheesecloth 4in wider than the height of the shade and long enough to fit around it, with an extra 1¹/²in as a seam allowance. Pin one end of the cheesecloth along a strut, leaving ³/⁴in at each end for a seam and gathering the fabric slightly as you go.

6 Pin the cheesecloth along the next strut and sew in place using blanket stitch. To sew blanket stitch, insert the needle behind the strut and pull it out in front. Do not pull all the wool through.

7 Take the needle through the loop of wool, then pull the wool tight. Continue stitching the cheesecloth to each strut in the same way until you reach the first pinned seam. When you reach the final strut, join the two edges and stitch them together.

8 Finish off the top and bottom of the shade by rolling the edges around the wire frame, then pin and stitch them in place. Ask an electrician to attach the light fixture to the tripod stand and then place the shade on top.

ECCENTRIC CREPE SHADE

Crêpe bandage is great material to work with. It has just enough stretch to give a good tight fit and the textured surface grips as you layer the bandage. Keep an even tension as you wind it around a wire frame and use hot glue if necessary at key points to prevent any slipping or sagging. Make sure you leave an opening at the top, however, to allow the heat to escape.

YOU WILL NEED
- ◆ copper bonsai-training wire
- ◆ wire cutters
- ◆ needle-nose pliers
- ◆ thinner wire
- ◆ glue gun with all-purpose glue sticks
- ◆ rolls of bandage

1 Cut three equal lengths of bonsai wire and bend each into three curves, using the pliers. The wire will straighten up when you release it, so exaggerate the shapes as you bend them.

2 Bind the three ends of the bonsai wire firmly together with the thinner wire. Be generous with the amount of wire because you need to make a solid fixture, and use the needle-nose pliers to help you to bind tightly.

3 Run a length of wire between the three struts, winding it around each strut, to form the lowest of three enclosing wires that will make the framework for the bandage binding.

4 Wind around two more lengths of wire to complete the framework.

5 Using the pair of needle-nose pliers, carefully twist the ends of the struts into curved "feet."

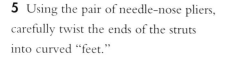

6 Apply hot glue to a strut about 2in down from the binding at the top of the framework and to one end of the bandage. Wrap the bandage tightly around the wire to attach it firmly.

7 Wrap the bandage around the framework, pulling it to get the tension right and applying hot glue whenever it crosses a strut.

8 Finally, glue and wrap a small length of bandage to cover the wire binding right at the top of the framework. Use the glue gun to seal the edge and be sure to leave a 2in gap around the top in order for the heat to escape.

Above: This frame was made in exactly the same way but butter muslin has been draped over it to give a lighter effect.

Opposite: The different layers and angles of the bandage wrapping show up in a subtle pattern of light and dark shapes when you light the shade with a small spotlight.

PINK-TISSUE SHADE

This brilliant pink-paper lamp shade will make a stunning centerpiece for a room and will cast a flattering pink light over everything at the same time. Make the size of the lamp shade appropriate for your room. Since it is very lightweight, it can be made quite big, which is useful if your house has high ceilings. Attach equal lengths of chain to the curled hooks and hang the light fixture in the center, so that the heat rises out of the top of the shade.

YOU WILL NEED
- ◆ bonsai-training wire
- ◆ wire cutters
- ◆ thinner wire
- ◆ needle-nose pliers
- ◆ chains to hang the shade
- ◆ glue gun with all-purpose glue sticks
- ◆ bright pink, good-quality tissue paper
- ◆ water-based varnish
- ◆ paintbrush

1 Cut three equal lengths of bonsai wire for the struts. Bend them into wavy shapes. You can exaggerate the shape since the wire will spring back a bit. Bind the ends together with thinner wire, using needle-nose pliers.

2 Attach a length of the thinner wire about 4³/4in from the end of one strut, winding it around to secure it. Then take it around the other two struts in the same way. This will form the top of the framework. Wind around two more wires in the same way.

3 Using the pliers, curl the ends of the struts where the chains will be attached. Apply glue to one of the struts, and fold the edge of a piece of tissue paper over it. Stretch the tissue across, and glue it to the next strut.

4 Continue in this way overlapping where necessary, until the framework is covered. Wind and glue a strip around the point where the three struts are joined. Brush on a coat of varnish to tighten up the paper and bond the layers.

MATERIALS

Each of the projects featured in the book has its individual materials list. The tools that are used most frequently are the glue gun and the cordless electric drill. Other useful tools are the wire cutters, needle-nose pliers and staple gun.

There are many different types of paintbrush. You should use small household paintbrushes for large areas of color and applying varnish and size, and soft artist's brushes for more detailed work. The man-made fiber brushes are very good, and it is best to have at least three different sizes: one fine-pointed, one medium-pointed and one square-tipped brush. Brushes should be thoroughly cleaned after use.

Water-based paints dispense with the need for solvents and different sorts can be mixed together to intensify the colors, but never mix oil-based paint with a water-based type. You can use undiluted white glue as a varnish or any other water-based varnish. Shellac is used to seal bare wood. It contains a solvent and is very quick drying.

When covering lamp shades, it is a good idea to shine a light behind the fabric or paper that you plan to use to check what the effect will be. If you want a general glow, then go for a material that allows light to shine through. If you want a darker effect use a less permeable material. Craft shops sell frames in all shapes and sizes, and there are many accessories that hold the shade safely away from the bulb. It is very important for lamps and shades to be stable, and one of these special fixtures will provide that reassurance.

Wallpaper paste (1); paper mesh (2); lamp shade trivet (3); bonsai wire (4); wood veneer sheets (5); handmade inlaid paper (6); white glue (7); tape measure (8); scissors (9); wire cutters (10); colored tissue paper (11); hole punch (12); cheesecloth (13); size (14); shellac (15); Dutch metal leaf (16); thread (17); pins (18); household paintbrush (19); broad square-tipped artist's brush (20); fine artist's brush (21); pencil (22); glue gun (23); staple gun (24); glass paints (25); ruler (26); brown wrapping paper (27); scalpel (28); sandpaper (29); steel wool (30); crêpe bandage (31); corrugated cardboard (32).

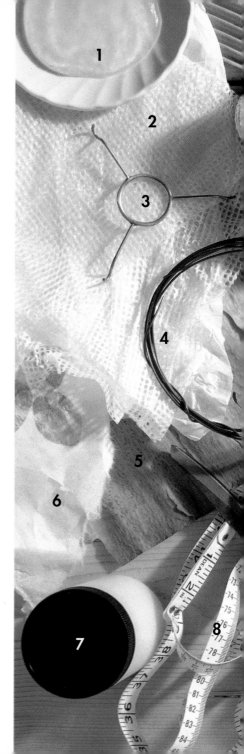

TECHNIQUES

All of the projects in the book are easy to make, but there are a couple of even simpler ways to transform lamp shades and bases which are well worth knowing.

Trimming shade edges

Notion stores sell a wide range range of dressmaking trimmings, many of which are suitable for dressing up simple lamp shades. A fringed or beaded edging can be glued in place to transform a plain shade. To get the best results, you will need to seal the ends of the trimming once it has been cut to size to prevent them from fraying. This can be done by turning a small seam back and slip stitching it flat. If you do not have a needle and thread, paint the ends with clear nail polish.

1 Measure the length of trimming needed to go around the shade plus a small seam allowance at each end. Stitch the seams flat to prevent the raw edges from fraying.

2 Heat the glue gun and apply some glue to the surface of the shade. Attach the trimming immediately. You will get an instant bond since the hot glue cools on contact. If you are working with very fine trimmings, it may be neater to stitch the trimmings on to the shade.

Lamp shade lacing

One of the simplest ways to adorn a lamp shade is to lace the edges. To calculate the length of lacing required, measure around the top and bottom of the shade, then add the two measurements together and multiply this figure by two and a half.

1 Using scissors, cut a strip of cardboard to use as a spacer to mark the positions of the holes around the top and bottom edges of the shade.

3 Attach one end of the string to the inside of the shade using the glue gun or a dab of all-purpose glue.

Working with old lamp bases

Natural wood or previously painted lamp bases are perfect to work with. Here are two simple techniques for renovating them.

A stony surface

Many lamp bases are made from smooth-glazed pottery and simply applying a new coat of paint does not often produce a pleasing finish. One of the best ways to transform these lamps is by adding a stony surface.

2 Set the punch to the required hole size and make a hole at each mark.

4 Lace the string in and out of the holes. Cut the string when you reach the end, and secure it at the back with a dot of glue. Repeat with the other line of punched holes.

1 Paint the lamp base with your chosen color of latex paint. Mix equal amounts of paint and white glue in a bowl. Then stir in roughly the same volume of sand. Make this mixture in sufficient quantity to cover the surface of the base – probably about a cupful.

2 Paint the gritty mixture all over the lamp base and allow it to dry.

3 Lighten the mixture with white latex paint and stroke this lighter color over the base, but do not cover all the last coat of paint.

Gilding

Gilding a lamp base with Dutch metal leaf will give a warm reflective gold surface that is far superior to the finish you get from paints.

1 Paint the lamp with size. Allow to dry until just tacky, normally for about a half hour.

2 Cut strips of leaf on its backing paper. Press them onto the tacky surface and rub the backing paper to transfer the gold. Keep adding until all the size is covered.

3 Use a pad of fine wool to rub off the excess gold leaf. This will not remove the leaf that has adhered to the size so you can rub quite hard.

4 Finally, paint on a coat of white polish to protect the gilding. It will not dull the glimmer of the surface.

TEMPLATES

The templates and patterns in this book can be used to any size. The easiest way to enlarge the templates is on a photocopier. If you do not have access to a photocopier, they can be enlarged using a grid system. Trace the template and draw a grid of evenly spaced squares over your tracing. To scale up, draw a larger grid on to another piece of paper. Copy the outline on to the second grid by taking each square individually and drawing the relevant part of the outline in the larger square. Finally, draw over the lines to make sure they are continuous. When tracing templates, you will need a pencil, tracing paper, white paper or graph paper and scissors.

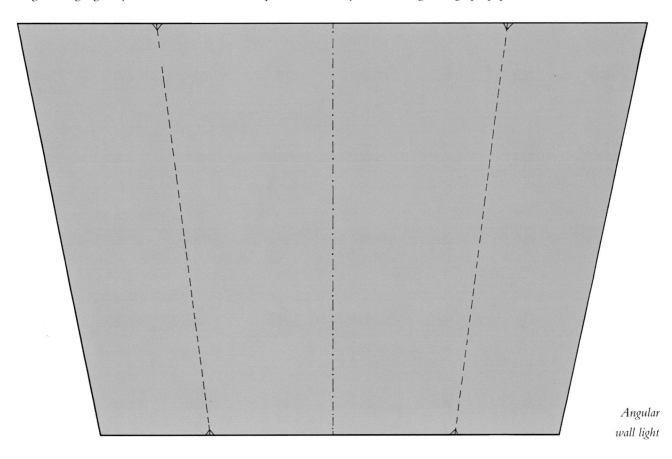

*Angular
wall light*

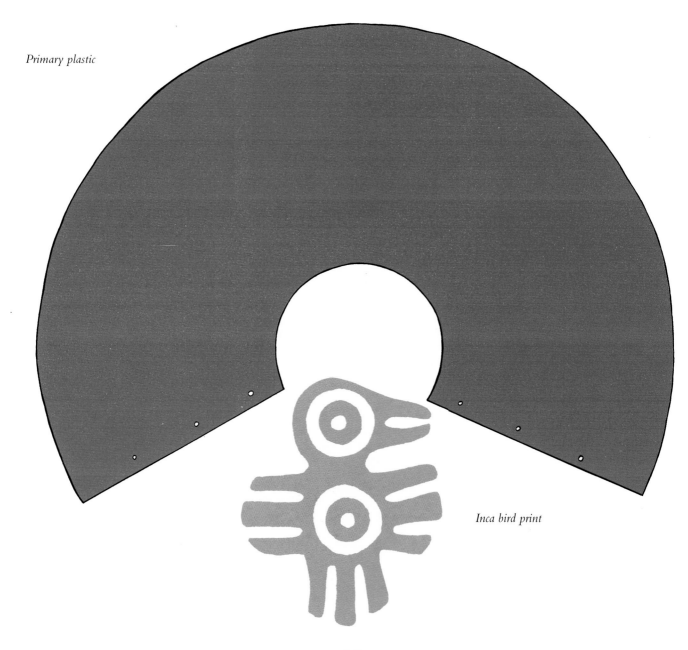

Primary plastic

Inca bird print

Primary plastic

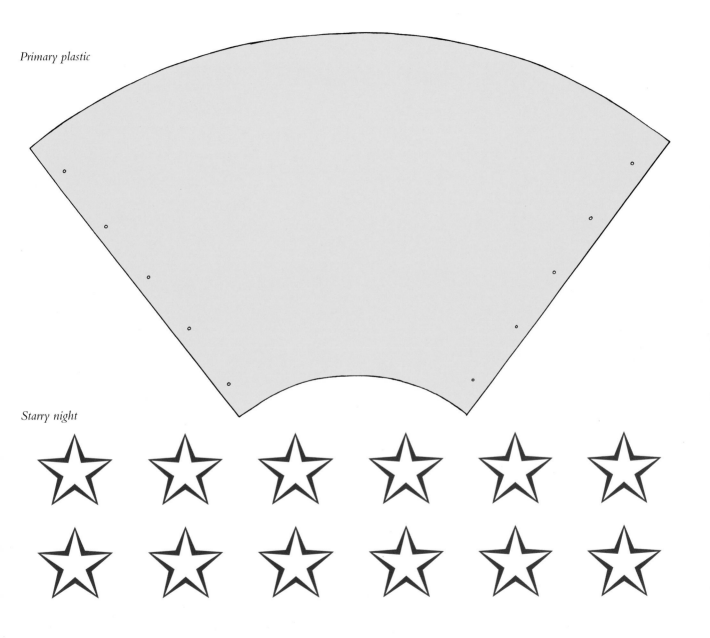

Starry night

SAFETY NOTE

The projects and ideas suggested in this book are for making
decorative lamp shades and bases. The emphasis throughout is on
style and special effects rather than the nuts and bolts of electrical
wiring, which is not a suggested do-it-yourself area.

Electricity can be lethal, and we suggest that you consult a
qualified electrician for anything beyond the rewiring of
a plug or changing of a fuse.

Always shut off a light and remove the plug from the socket
before attempting to remove or attach a shade.

Make sure all lamp shades and fabrics are a safe distance from bulbs.
They do generate heat which can cause some materials to ignite if
they are in prolonged contact or even too close. Never exceed
the recommended wattage for the fixture as this could cause
plastic to melt or wiring to overheat.

If you buy an old lamp, it is advisable to have the fixture and
wiring completely replaced. A professional electrician will do this
for you. Old plugs and wiring do not meet modern safety
standards so spend the extra money to be on the safe side.

Never leave lit candles unattended in a room since they are a
potential fire hazard. Better to put them out and relight them
when you are present to enjoy their glow.

INDEX

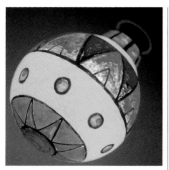
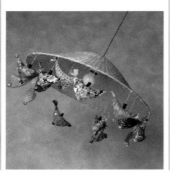

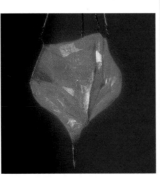

Acknowledgements
The authors and publishers
would like to thank Sacha
Cohen, Josh George and Sam
Walton for their enthusiasm and
hard work, and M & F Products
(Croydon) Ltd for loaning the
lamp shade frames and fittings
used in this book: